RHYMES WITH HYENAS

RHYMES WITH HYENAS

HEATHER TAYLOR-JOHNSON

RECENT
WORK
PRESS

Rhymes with Hyenas
Recent Work Press
Canberra, Australia

Copyright © Heather Taylor-Johnson, 2021

ISBN: 9780645008982 (paperback)

A catalogue record for this
book is available from the
National Library of Australia

Cover image: Diana Akmetianova via unsplash
Cover design: Recent Work Press
Set by Recent Work Press

recentworkpress.com

PL

For Alison Flett and Rachael Mead

Biographies

Ursula Brangwen has been shortlisted for the Blake Prize in Poetry and longlisted for the Peter Porter. She is the author of two full-length poetry collections and one chapbook. Ursula is as indebted to D.H. Lawrence for writing *Women in Love*, where she met her husband, Rupert, as she is to Rhymes with Hyenas for encouraging her voice to shine through.

Gudrun Brangwen is an artist presently teaching English in Tokyo. She has never lived in Australia, but she is widely read in its poetry. Unlike her sister, Ursula, Gudrun works hard to distance herself from her former character in D.H. Lawrence's *Women in Love*.

Caddy Compson was once the focus of William Faulkner's *The Sound and the Fury*, though her narrative was not told by her. The three male narrators, her brothers Benjy, Quentin and Jason, were so moved by her sexuality that it was a point of mania, ultimately leading to castration, suicide and lifelong bitterness. She is an exile from Jefferson, Mississippi, where her family and her daughter live. Caddy now lives in Adelaide with her partner and their two young boys, who inspire many of her poems. Her first Australian publication was in *Rabbit*.

Dolores Haze might be known to most as the paedophile Humbert Humbert's 'Lolita' in Vladimir Nabokov's book by the same name, but she'd rather be known as a spoken word artist. She has competed nationally in SLAM competitions and in 2018 received an Arts SA grant to travel to America to perform and compete. She visited her hometown in Ramsdale while there with her daughter, Bea, and is currently writing a memoir about it. Dolores thanks Rhymes with Hyenas for helping her tighten her poems on the page.

Mel Isaacs is a South African actor, dancer and a playwright who has travelled the world with her stage productions since 2017. She hopes the poems she wrote with Rhymes with Hyenas are reason enough to now add 'poet' to her list of titles. Mel would like to stop writing about David Lurie, her professor / abuser in J.M. Coetzee's *Disgrace*, but the tiny poems keep coming. Perhaps she'll adapt them into a play one day.

Lilith is a former First Lady, Adam's first wife from Hebrew Mythology. Refusing to lie beneath him, Lilith was exiled from Eden, only to make room for Eve, Adam's second wife who later became Lilith's. Lilith and Eve were together for a millennium until Eve's death in 2019. Lilith is the author of *The Moon at the Finish Line*, shortlisted for the Anne Elder Award, and *My Body in the Way*. She has won the Josephine Ulrick Prize and been shortlisted three times for the Newcastle Poetry Prize. *Not Truth*, a hybrid work exploring the space between rumours and truth and between prose and poetry, will be published by Giramondo later this year. Meanwhile, she continues to write poems about Eve.

Katherina Minola is otherwise known as Kate, in William Shakespeare's *The Taming of the Shrew*, though she would never sign that name to a poem and she would never again say the sun was the moon. Katherina takes inspiration from Rhymes with Hyenas and runs monthly poetry workshops for female refugees. Her first poetry collection will be out with Wakefield Press in 2022.

Dear friends,

I hope you don't find me too forward for contacting all of you at once, especially as some of you don't know each other, but I have an idea, perhaps an outlandish one considering our varying origins and dispositions, but don't they seem to be the ideas which so often work? Rupert and I rent a shack in Moonta Bay, lack of noise seems to be what we need, to be outside in the day and inside at night. He is sick, chronically, and I will do whatever I can for him. My husband is the kind of person who wishes to be perceived as tragic so perhaps this new, slow devastation suits him. It does not, however, suit me. I try to be patient and attentive and I do think I'm managing the caring 'role' well, I do think I am able to be a strong and loving partner, but I tend to pity myself on occasion and must find a way through it. I feel it would be good for me to have women in my life right now so I have attached a poem, and this, you see, is my idea: that we might meet once in a while and share our poetry and woes and celebrate life's small splendours. We are all, after all, literary beasts.

Yours,
Ursula

Today, a Crab

-Ursula

Low tide distances
with an enviable aloofness.
By these ochre rocks I hide
from wind and children,
tiny crustaceans only getting by,
my own footprints and other
natural distractions.
The sea will move and churn life,
sense just when to ease back
receding into its own self-worth.
There is nothing to prove -
not to sandal holders, these clouds,
the far reaches of the ice continent
which blows this wind
        this day my way.

Not even birds can carry the sea from itself.

This is our marriage
a sweetness of habitation,[1]
today the coast of South Australia.
Convalescence has its privileges:
the stillness of a lain-in bed,
shapes of our bodies come to rest
as if we were finally home.
Forgive me my brooding, the crinkle of my contemplations,
the distance I cover to hold your hand
but you accept demise as if brought to you
by this very low tide.
        Today, a crab
purple and hard in the strong sun
still wet underneath where it is blue and soft.

---

1 Lawrence, DH. Women in Love. (1950 ed) New York: Viking Press,
  1920 p 371

Claw to claw it was the length of my torso
gripping at my cleaving chest,
sightless eyes popping
like two buds toward light.
It had seen enough of the unrealised world; [2]
it had triumphed over everything. [3]
In the hard packed shore
it found a grave
        yet I can do nothing but bring you tea.
        I must learn to be more like the sea.

Our bed, your breath, caged, it flutters
madly to escape, then falters, then
falls. I hardly sleep anymore.
In the morning you allow the sun
its goodness into your English skin,
the salt to clear your head of things
which only make you heavy.
We laze, I to be nearer to your weight,
to be nearer the earth and your imprint upon it.
Life has afforded us this—the will to wither, to carry on,
this sea, these gulls playing overhead
as if our story were torn and scattered
        pieces of bread.

---

2   ibid
3   ibid

I'm so happy that we met at that little bookshop in Glenelg, Ursula! I'll tell you all that I'm not very good at poetry but I write almost every day, little things that might not seem important but I love this idea and I'm a BIG YES. I see Dolores is on the list. I know her! Would you believe that just the other night we were talking about workshopping our poetry? Maybe that means this group is written in the stars. Or the blank page. Here's two short ones from me. I can only meet in the daytime until Fringe is over. My friends and I are performing a little play we wrote called 'Shambles' in the Spiegeltent. Come and check us out!
Cheers, Mel

Adelaide 1

-Mel

Big days, streets unfold.
We breathe the air

as if we deserve it –
make love in hidden places.

Adelaide 2

-Mel

A stride is the length
of latitude between our feet
and attitude.

Hi to everyone. I love this idea and thank you for thinking of me, but first, Ursula, I am so sorry for Rupert and you. Goodness knows I've understood since I was young how taxing caring can be. Rewarding and necessary, as well, to be sure. I'm still new to Adelaide, its vowels and ocean and wine-based etiquette, and being a stay-at-home mother without much support gets pretty tough around the edges and sticky inside the intricate lace so yes, it would be wonderful to meet regularly with a group of women. I'm not sure how long we plan to be here (Jean-Guy's job, always Jean-Guy's job—he's in Abu Dhabi now ☹) but I think I can commit to a year. Am I getting ahead of myself? It's an issue with me. How many times has it gotten me into trouble? I'd love to talk poetry but I'll have to bring the little one. He's only five months so we're attached at either the hip or the breast. I hope no one minds.

I've attached a poem called 'Exiting an Aircraft for the 83rd Time'. Will we give feedback or just share?

Where should we meet and how often?

We should think of a name ☺

Yes, yes,
Caddy

Dear Caddy and everyone,
I am sure I speak for us all when I say we're happy to have him along. If we can't support one another, we'll fail as a poetry group and we'll fail as women.
Yours,
Ursula

Exiting an Aircraft for the 83rd Time

-Caddy

I long for a river to greet my body as I dive like a virgin
into sex and rise from her waters a woman.
Twenty-two hours of in-flight entertainment
and compartmentalised meals in trays
and I am standing in Australia
other side of this impossible world.
An airplane rises in front of me
its shadow slicing the sea.

My feet are light, free from the deep rootedness
that is my America and all she holds—
crush of dew, scent of soil, ripple song—
still my body weighs me down.
I swear the sun is hotter here.
Is it possible it could be closer?
I swallow hard.
Immediately dry out.

Hello again. Last night my older son and I were playing with his stuffed meerkat and I started thinking that meerkats live in a matriarchal society so if we wanted a name we could be the Meerkat Muses. It's silly but it made me smile.

His loving mother,

Caddy

Dear all,

Animals are good. I know bonobos form a matriarchal society where females bond together to overcome males. Rather harsh, but interesting.

Yours,

Ursula

Clown fishes are matriarchal. Or is the plural clown fish? They begin as males but mature into females and if a female dies a male fills in by becoming female. Gender fluid, baby! I also learned that the Kaurna people see the sun as female and the moon as male, which is different, right? And Tindo (sun woman) eats fish when she sits in darkness. Not that I can think how it'd fit into our group but just saying.

Cheers, Mel

Dear all of us / This sounds good. I've been working on sonnet sequences for the last few months and liking the project, so I'll go from there. Be warned, they're more playful than what usually comes out of me, dare I say puerile, so they feel rather minor right now. Of course I'm of the mind to make them something major. As most of you probably know I recently lost my partner Eve, so beware that she is in everything I write these days. Yes, I agree, women need women.

I could meet once a month, and not to be pushy but can I add in a rule of one-poem-only? It would be difficult for me to read more than one poem per person. When would I ever have time to write? We could get into bylaws such as 'Mel's two poems are very short so they could just count as one poem' but one should never underestimate the power of a short poem. And so now you will cringe because I'm submitting a long one, and by all means, critique. Let's be fierce about our poetry, treat it with dignity. We could meet at Bliss on Bent St off Rundle. It's an organic café so we can avoid the back and forth emails concerning vegetarianism and gluten free and the odd proclivity for raw food (etc etc, the last one was a joke). I choose a café over someone's house because from what I can tell we're fairly spread out between the Hills and the Fleurieu and York Peninsulas, so central would be best. First day of autumn? I love autumn in Adelaide. My lungs love autumn in Adelaide. The fires are so awful right now that I might just take a second to dream of autumn air.

I'm sorry but I will never be a Bonobo Poet. Bonobos are a highly sexual breed and I feel as women we're sexualised enough on a daily fucking basis. Also, a meerkat is cute. Do we want to be a group of cuteness? And Tindo was created by Teendo yerle, who's an all-powerful male, so we certainly don't want to go there. Unfortunately I have nothing to offer regarding the name at the moment. Will think on it.

And dear Ursula, I am so sorry to hear about the change in yours and Rupert's life. Strength to you both / Lilith

Eve's Second Sin

-Lilith

1. *What You Ask*

You ask can there be forgiveness.
Dare I care in this desert
where dust crusts the cracks in my eyes
and windblown earth picks pox in my skin
browned by days and years?
And dare I care if forgiveness comes
after years of exile without a trial
after Adam's denial and God's last word?
Dare I hope for Heaven someday?
Perhaps I'll just keep on my way.

Eve, all these years
and still you ask among this dirt?
I spit at the roots of the Native Pine
so that it may thrive. The sun's in my eyes.

2. *What the Native Pine Saw*

On the morning of our first day
ahead, South Australia
the air sitting still, straddling your back
pulling you down while my heart grows up.
I kiss sorrow weeping from your lashes
as I kiss the serpent's purple tongue.
You turn to me as if to say
Is this the way?

Eve, your skin is smooth and fair,
here is a garland for your hair:
dead cicadas I found at my feet.
I'll cup your breast in return.
Look how you open
now that man is just a word.

3. *The Furthest Dune*

Eve, the sun is rising
and I see the sweat above your lips.
Will we be there soon?
It's just over the furthest dune.

You are a form born of man's bone
flesh of his flesh, you hadn't a choice.
My voice wasn't supposed to be heard,
thunder scratched from a lightning bolt.
I left grasping clumps of earth
I will not lie beneath!
because I would not lie beneath.
Find your voice today and the days that will follow and follow
until we reach the furthest dune, hand in hand
feet covered in sand, dead cicadas humping our hair.

4. *Stone Pillows*

Eve, I know your feet ache
and would if you could turn back to bathe
once more, for hours, in Eden's lake
but trust my steps beside your steps
this sound pace moving west.

Soon we will rest?

Enough—
this desert is raptors circling above.
Eve, my love, you know knowledge, you know shame
know Adam is a prick plucked from dust and Eve, my love
after the knowledge after the shame
know that Adam is only a name.
Rest with me now on these pillows of stone.
Under the stars we're almost alone.

5. The Blooming Milky Way

Under the stars (another world of other gods
you will one day know) we are alone.
You dream of waterfalls and zebras
wonder if anything has changed back home.
Would women yet be able to conceive
without their Adam to their Eve?

Me, I would not go back, even in dreams.
I would not go back, I would not
go, I would not, I would not –
and so we are walking, our hips the softest of cogs
our lazy fingers drooping with swollen blood.
Listen, we count heartbeats instead of minutes
kilometres better measured by the sun.
Our footprints are for the world to see just how far we've come.

Good morning to all this Valentine's Day and with this email
I choose to celebrate poetry and women—apt, wouldn't you
agree? In lieu of flowers or a card I offer you the hyena. I did
some research last night and hyenas are also of a matriarchal
society, and they are strong. Even the smallest female hyena
has more influence than the male. They are supreme hunters
and protective parents and have multipurpose clitorises
which allow them to urinate, mate and give birth. I would
love to add my friend Katherina to the list. If she is up for
the challenge, I think you will enjoy her as a person and a
poet. Please let me know, Ursula, if you have any objections.
I understand it could be a numbers game and don't want to
ruin your vision. And Mel, I will book tickets for your opening
night, if anyone should wish to join me. / Lilith

> Dear friends,
> Thank you for your sympathy, Lilith, and please do add
> Katherina. I like the idea of the hyena, a misrepresented and
> powerful creature.
> Yours,
> Ursula

The Laughing Hyenas?
Cheers, Mel

> Hyenas laugh when they are nervous so I don't think we
> should call ourselves that. We could be the Rhyming Hyenas,
> who needn't rhyme at all. And so it is after midnight, no
> longer VD. / Lilith

> > Late to this thread. 'Rhymes with Hyenas'. I've
> > got a teenage daughter so might not need more
> > oestrogen in my life but I want life to be less
> > about what we need than what we want so I've
> > attached a poem for you. It's anxious.
> > Dolores

Computer

-Dolores

The shame of eating over the keyboard.
The smudge I left when I peeled off a sticker.
The opened mail next to the screen.
The television in my peripheral.
The hum that is there & the budding words.
The backspace mocking, the bright blue
& brighter white, the whiskey sour
the yellow lighter, the photos & the messaging
the distance we cross, the breadth of our lives
the blood of my poetry dormant inside.
Fear of hackers & global warming.

Rhymes with Hyenas: 'subpoenas'
Cheers, Mel

My Wieners?
Dolores

Rhymes with Hyenas. I love the name. I saw your poem
in Cordite, U—congratulations. / Lilith

Dear Rhymes with Hyenas,
If you ever decide to bring your daughter,
Dolores, we'd be grateful for some
teenage angst to ground our poetry in its
true roots, which carries the chords of
the blues and the rhythm of jazz, if I am
correct. And thank you, Lilith. I am happy
to have placed it.
Yours,
Ursula

Hello everyone and thanks for inviting me. Life is so confusing and I don't
know how to make sense of my poetry so go gently on me but then I also
think we should be brutal, as Lilith said, because what good is anything if
there is no truth and in my experience truth is brutal. And wine, I'll need
wine, there is no wine at Bliss. I've never shared my writing before except
with Lilith and it was only once and I was timid so apologies to you, Lilith,
but the poem I've attached is the one you've read. I'm not spontaneous so
I'd like to stick with this poem until I understand what it is I'm trying to do
and only then can I move on. It's such hard work, I'm afraid I'm hard work,
maybe a group of hyenas can help me with all of it, maybe?
All the best, Katherina (some of you only know me as Kate—please don't
call me Kate)

Morning

-Katherina

Only slightly hungover:
fug.

Heat burns the brick   and bakes us
          air conditioning drones, ear canal, squint
I drink milk from the carton –
                              I eat nuts from a jar

Bathrobe drugged:
fug.

Dear friends,
If we're to go by the first day of autumn,
as suggested by Lilith, I will see you cackle
in a month, though I'd prefer if we met sooner.
The sunset tonight overfloweth.
Yours,
Ursula

I agree—a month feels way too
far away now that I've read all the
poems. Colour me pumped, I've
attached a poll for us to vote on a
date. Don't take this to mean I'm
going to organise heaps of other
things. I'm for reading the poems
in advance & coming prepared to
critique.
Dolores

Critique and comradery, so convivial. And of course,
Katherina, I will drink with you. And "cackle"—a group of
hyenas. Well done on setting us straight, Ursula. In regards to
the sunset, we've become death worshipers, for it's the fires
making our sunsets so beautiful. / Lilith

Is anyone finding it hard to breathe?
I don't want my children or dog outside at all ☹
Not coping,
Caddy

My asthma is killing me!
Mel

A Good Day

-Caddy

Are you aware outside the sun yawns? These minutes of dawn
anticipate the world: breakfast, the shoes, transport, money—
all things linear before noon.

Bubbles never hurt a soul,
the round outer rind of them, how the hand slips in,
the tight gasps, dozens of pops, the slow slide of a plate

and skin on skin I have the run of his leg, his foot
on my lips; he gets a clean bottom and I get his eyes,
recognition of him in me, me in him

and later, just for a moment, I close my eyes, pretend I'm walking
through a heavy forest with unfallen rain and the rising green
and then I lie in the grass among bugs and sleep, and sleep

then strip garlic smooth and bare and chop it up
only to stop and lick my fingers
pretend I am cooking for God

and finally, when the sun is gone, darkness will clothe us
as we shrug off the day with thundering shudders.
Nothing more than tiny aftershocks of ancient earthquakes,
quakes we bear, quakes we hold.

Dear Caddy,

I was charmed by your enthusiasm at our meeting. You are an inspiration, having come with printed copies of your next offering. So organised. I didn't want to wait until our meeting to tell you how much I relished 'A Good Day', so fecund with Bruno's nappies and forest dreaming, that balance of the domestic and exotic; it made me ache. The pain I feel when I think about not being able to have a child is so far inside my gut it's where I begin. It's real, the 'clock'. I hadn't felt it before when a baby had wanted to come and I fear I've now missed my chance. It's such a hard word: 'clock'. Your Bruno is a gem. He slotted well into the role of Rhymes with Hyenas' honorary male member, and oh what a poet he will grow to be! So with that, don't let what Lilith said about the shape of his head worry you (slightly rude). We will worship his little toes and his head. She's a good poet though and I enjoy the way she digs in with the critiques (she is an academic, in case you haven't caught on), but her comment on my rhyming was odd as she clearly uses rhyme herself. I've had a long think about my 'sea' and 'tea' and 'way' and 'day' and I believe our rhymes are equal in their intent. I don't think it's the rhyming, as she said, that makes my lines 'practiced' but perhaps the indentation, or the indentation and the rhyming as complements to one another (and detriments to us all). Still, I am loath to take them out.

Yours,

Ursula

Hi Ursula. It's sometimes embarrassing how organised I am, I just thank goodness I can laugh at myself. I'm glad you brought up Lilith. Must say I was a tiddy-bit intimidated. I hate that we're talking behind her back, or typing, I suppose. I was trying to work out how to leave Bruno at home next time but who would look after those fingers and that head? Jean-Guy is home on Sundays but he says it's too difficult to have both children with him alone, especially as he can't get Bruno to take a bottle. I find juggling the domestic so hard so thank you for your email. And Ursula, I stand by my words, *I love rhymes*. And the indentations! Here's me sending a brava kiss your way. Those are roses at your feet. I don't do much with indentations but I should because they're fun to read and you placed us at a beach for goodness sake, we should at least be allowed some fun 😊 Go with your gut, that womanly gut where fire sometimes pauses to reflect on itself (we are all still thinking about fire, aren't we? Have they really stopped? Are they coming back? Will next year be worse?). And yes, she did rhyme, of course. What lasts most for me when I think about Lilith at the meeting is not her obvious annoyance with Bruno (because he was demanding my attention a lot and that really was annoying) but the story she told us of the women in the Amazon breastfeeding monkeys and also the one about the 22 Souliot women throwing their children from crags before they jumped, one by one, singing 'Death above slavery! Set our bodies free!' Have a lovely Tuesday in this beautiful sun,
Caddy

What did you think of the first meeting?
D

Intimidating? Wonderful?
xMel

Want more.
D

'Swinging cantinas'
xMel

Tina Arenas
xD

Katherina / Yesterday was superb, don't you think? I went to bed feeling very nourished, very connected. I thought everyone brought something utterly unique to the table—patience, exuberance, realism, control. You brought a fresh wisdom. You offered questioning and philosophy. You were a blooming marvel, Katherina. Thoughts from you? / Lilith

I agree about the meeting. It felt big to me and I wrote when I got home. Something fit for the bin, something *overdone* but at least I wrote when I got home and kept writing, first poetry then some tirade that I'll call memoir so it sounds sane when really it was madness reflecting my circumstances. Petrucio didn't come home, who cares, I didn't go to bed until after 3 and when I woke up I had the strangest craving for a schnitzel, really intense and it took everything I had to wait until the pub started serving lunch so I'm asking you, is there a correlation between writing and greasy pub food? All the best, Katherina

The Pub

-Lilith

1. The Pub

The flies are lazy on the bottle's rim
and the unsuspecting finger
on the walls and taps
and looking at reflections
in the dust-streaked mirror.

The man drinks VB in the bright
green can, because *grass is green*
and *water does flow* and *once
there was a wife in Wagga*, maybe.

His mates laugh without him
in their fourday stubble
and their stubbies with their rollies
and their dirt-protected skin.

It's thirty-nine degrees inside.

2. The Pub

My love with the white down
down the nape of her soft white neck
and soft to the small of her downy back
holds the baby roo.
*So lovely, yes;
only passing through.*

The bartender takes a shot of whiskey
straight from Tennessee
wonders why in Daly Waters
            while

the black man wanders as he drinks

stumbling through old daydreams.
The whitefellas say he wandered in the womb
and *christalmightyhewontstandstill*.

3. The Pub

Another bus rushes in, my love shows off the roo
while the toilet seat heats up the loo
travellers grunting and coughing while

the bartender pops tops of beer
for backpacking Yanks and Germans
and pies and pasties everywhere
like Japanese and Dutch, and the orders
from Brits and South Africans
for fish and bloody chips fly in

twenty minutes barely enough
for this kind of culture.

They eye the Aboriginal man.

Speak in other languages.

Leave as quickly as they came.

Ursula / What a wonderful launch last night of
the anthology—you should be very pleased with
yourself having such a stunning poem in there.
Michelle Cahill's opening one struck me deeply.
She's very careful with words and her use of
commas is enviable. Tell me what you think
when you get around to reading / responding.
And very happy to see our own Louise Nicholas
and Natalie Harkin in the mix—Adelaide poets
do know how to make a splash on occasion.
I had far too much fun last night with this new
cackle of friends and suddenly there we were
at the Austral, danger of one of my colleague's
university days. Oh yes, I'd been warned,
and still I went. I should have entered those
doors wearing a t-shirt that read 'If you see
me smoking a cigarette tell me it's time to go
home'. I've been making up t-shirt slogans in my
head ever since Mel showed up at our meeting
wearing 'You should see my library'.
I'm crawling into bed to spend this rainy
Saturday reading the rest of the anthology,
picking up where I left off with Libby Hart. I like
her very much. Eve and I had read her first book
together, cuddled in bed, a beautiful memory
now engrained on every page of that book. Must
re-read it someday. Or perhaps not. / xLilith

Dear Lilith,
Thank you for your email. It was lovely
to see you at the launch. Wasn't the
welcome to country especially good,
bringing in storytelling? Sometimes I
worry us white folk are simply giving lip
service when we do that (how to play a
role in reconciliation if I can't trust the do-
gooders' intentions?) but this one felt true
and meaningful. The Austral isn't a place I
would ever choose to go so I had to shun

the suggestion. Besides, I can't bear to leave Rupert for too long, and it's a good thing I came home when I did. He had a terrible night and I'm glad I was by his side when he woke in fright, shat himself then cursed the world.

I, too, love Libby Hart. I once tried using her poems as inspiration for my own but they didn't come out very well. They're not worth sending through to the Hyenas, though equally not worth throwing out the door. Time will tell.

Yours
Ursula

Jeez Louise, Mel, thank you for putting me in a taxi last night after the Austral! I had to express a thousand and one toxins from my breasts as soon as I got home. Seriously, I had too much fun, and you just made me laugh and laugh. My stomach muscles are still feeling it. Weren't you talking about moving to Uruguay at some point? As vague as that conversation is, I woke up thinking about what a fine place Uruguay would be for an RWH meeting 😊
Hugs and a kiss and a bit of a hangover,
Caddy

Last night WAS a blast! Who'd have thought book launches could be so fun? Is that normal? All that wine? I did talk about moving to Uruguay next year, fingers crossed. You told me you'd miss me and the 'fleshy streets of Adelaide' would miss me. I actually wrote it down in my journal when I was alone on the loo because it sounded so nice I didn't want to forget it. Good luck with the hangover.
xMel

Thought I'd check in on you Katherina. Big discussion last night at the Austral. Drinks do that sometimes but I think we also gelled. You ok today? I don't get the highs & lows like you, just the lows & they stink of the past's red-hot shit & make me gag on the idea of my future, so I can relate to being sick in the present tense. If you keep trudging through the muck I'll squelch in it with you.
xD

Thanks Dolores, the hangover doesn't help but your words do.
All the best, Katherina

Dear Lilith,

Sorry for two emails in less than two hours, but I forgot to thank you for the acupuncture tip in my earlier email. I should have thought of it myself because it had worked brilliantly for a time with Rupert's pain. Unfortunately it didn't keep working, but I have seen the benefits and believe in the treatment. Now he uses marijuana. He's rather dependent on it, and I can't say I blame him, it seems to be such a tremendous help. Have you tried cannabis for your MS? I did some research this morning and it looks as though it has positive results. And on that, I am awfully sorry to hear about your diagnosis and really cannot believe I didn't mention that in my last email either. Perhaps I have too many things on my mind this morning (I don't in any way mean that to sound like a detraction from your health). You might find an essay by Gillian Mears to be of interest called 'Alive in Ant and Bee'. She had MS, of course. I cried when she died. Please do let me know anytime if there is anything I can do. As for now, I am about to make that acupuncture appointment. If it works, you shall be godmother.

Yours in friendship,

Ursula

Thank you for the kind words, Ursula. I have just discovered CBD oil, which you probably know is extracted from the cannabis plant. My body seems to react well to it and I'm glad it doesn't get me high. I'm not opposed to being stoned, mind you, just not when I'm working. Thank you also for the tip on the Mears essay. She is a treasure and her loss was deeply felt. And most of all, best of luck with the acupuncture. I do hope it provides. / Lilith (future Goddess Mother)

Sea Dragons

-Ursula

How deep this thirst?
I swallowed the ocean
      tasting of you
and like the velvety underbelly
of a stingray brushing
my bare legs kicking
in a sluggish rhythm

you took me by surprise
made me reflect on chance
and living as if I could die.
You were the water *and* the sky
all or nothing
always all.

I can't explain how love grows except for this –
lately when I swallow the ocean
      tasting of you
coral reefs cover my eyes,
sea dragons take harbour
in my body.
I give each one a name.

Mother

-Katherina

If my father was king:
then thistles   then knuckles   then rings

and prowess

then beneath she lay
     in velvet robes;
     between her legs

a rose.

My Vagina is not a Hole

-Dolores

My vagina is not a hole, empty with an aim to becoming full.
It doesn't need your impeding while trying to rest.
It's not a cave with dripping & cool connotations –
it is not damp; it doesn't echo.
Listen - it doesn't even know your name.

My vagina breathes its own inward outward rhythm
so subtle & secret I sometimes forget it's there
& when I remember, it comes flooding back.

More *yes* than *what*.
More *because* than *how*.

Katherina, you're shitting me—we both wrote
about vaginas? There's this thing called Spoke n
Slurred at the Coffee Pot off Rundle Mall every
month. It's a cool gig, cheap drinks & foul words
if you know what I mean. At the last one Kerryn
Tredrea read a poem about her vagina & dared
everyone to bring one next time. It's Thursday,
just in time to get the group's feedback & make
a few small edits. Come with me & we'll read
ours. Though I wonder if your structure would
transfer from page to stage? But then if spoken
word is performance & interpretation shouldn't
everything transfer from page to stage? What-
eva. I'm attaching an old poem just for you that's
sort of a vagina poem, vibing on the theme.
xDolores

I've never performed anything but
gender and sex though I'm often
emoldened by cheap drinks.
All the best, Katherina

I am not a Hole

-Dolores

Dr Rosen tells me I'm better.
It's the simple things you admire
       (my dog's tongue, for instance
       how it hangs when he runs so fast
       he loses his senses)
that help to make you whole.
I tell him *I am not a hole.*

He wants to send me to the stars;
I get acupuncture instead –
eight needles stimulate my feet & face
& calves & head & then I'm dead
asleep on the table, dreaming of insomnia.

My teenage daughter is having sex I say
       (her boyfriend's tongue, for instance
       how it hangs when he comes so fast
       he loses his senses).
Don't be a hole I think to her, pushing
on some pressure points while
Dr Rosen tells me I'm better.

Is it poor etiquette to rate our poems Dolores?
I don't really care about etiquette so I'll just tell
you that I like both your vagina poems better
than all the hyena poems so far, first meeting
and this upcoming one included. It seems I
prefer edgy poems and maybe that's why I've
found Caddy's annoying. This week's was too
much domesticity, no doubt before our time is
up she'll bring us one about her pet. I'm being
cruel which I don't really care about either but
I *am* being cruel so please don't tell anyone I
said this, most of all Caddy who literally *shines*.
Speaking of what a cow I am, Lilith lent me
Susan Hawthorne's book on cows which are
slaves, mythical, strong, meat. Is SH evoking
me? I think we should set ourselves the task of
writing a poem about hyenas.
Best, Katherina

Don't feel bad about being a cow—I love
cows. And you gotta admit, love em or
hate em, Caddy's poems are sensual. I bet
she's got a vagina poem.
xD

Instructions for my Husband

-Caddy

I feel it here, above my stomach
between the butterfly wings of my ribcage and central
like the universe, a longing for what's born of womb,
for broken children and sleeping children and children
who grow and don't. It's as if there is no containment
in this monthly bleed, no rules for patience, no rationale.
Hormones, you think, and stay clear of my sex while I
say to you: *stop telling me a glass half empty is a glass
half full*—just know that I am thirsty.

You weren't at the meeting Lilith and I didn't like it as much as I have before so really you can't go missing again ok? Are you alright?
Best, Katherina

hi, Katherina, thank you for checking in. I've been a brutal fucking mess, to be honest, but is that too honest? Talking about illness over and over feels both boring and solipsistic so I really shouldn't get started, but I find this whole MS business extremely isolating. It's very, very easy to feel out of touch with one's own friends so I appreciate your email immensely. / xLilith

By all means Lilith, dump on me so that one day I may dump on you.
Best, Katherina

Hi Lilith. We missed your feedback so much at the meeting! I hope you're ok? Aside from talking poetry we spent far too much time cursing the Catholic church, or maybe not enough. We toasted Mel when she gave us the news her show is going to Melbourne later in the year. Doesn't that make you want to sing? Dolores brought Bea, who was lost in her phone, but when spoken to she spoke back confidently enough for a 14-year-old, and she has the most genuine smile. Ursula was gaunt. I wish I could gift her a break ☹ Katherina wore sunglasses indoors and a scarf on her head. Some women can get away with extravagance, can't they? I wish I could without it looking like an inside joke. I was a little miserable, having only realised once I'd arrived that I'd caught my eldest's cold, but I'll survive.
Sniffly snotty,
Caddy

Dear Caddy / Thank you for checking on me. My body is not coping well with the changing weather and my mind seems to be following suit, but I too will survive. For now, at least. (A morbid thing to say, apologies.) Thank you for the update of the Hyenas. Such a lively bunch; so talented. Hope you and yours have gotten rid of the colds and are keeping well. / Lilith

Winter is coming, that's for sure. I keep staring at our potbelly stove, wondering how, when the time comes, I'll cope with lighting it and keeping it lit all day. There's something primal in knowing I'll be taking care of my children with flame that I made happen, but it's another chore, isn't it? I hope you're at least getting good rest. Are you at least getting good rest?
Sending you love,
Caddy

Insomnia, Caddy, but nothing new. Sending you love back / Lilith

Dear Hyenas / Sorry I missed the
meeting, have had a horrible week
of health and just exhausted, just
exhausted. I've been writing letters
to old friends, which is taking
the place of poems for now, and
thinking about letters and reading
about them as art. Madam de
Sévigné paints a lively picture of
being a woman in 17th century
France in her letters and I find
comfort knowing that now there
is us, doing an equally brilliant
job through emails in 21st century
Tarntanya Adelaide.
I have nothing new to offer for our
next meeting but I have dug up an
old poem I keep editing and re-
editing and am thinking perhaps it's
time to workshop it. Not a sonnet—
you get a break. / xLilith

Good luck with the rest of the
week, Lilith.
xxMel

Dearest Lilith,
I am sending you a care package today which may or may not hold a letter
for you.
All my love,
Ursula

Reaching

-Lilith

Somebody died three houses down
it was the girl—and this is what I want to say—
she was sixteen and could not breathe,
air failed to travel its path and floated
just beyond her reach. She could not speak
and worst of all, no one heard her reaching.

                Silence is never silence;
                darkness and cloud-cover cushion volume
                but they are not impassable.
                I sat outside; no wind carried the pain
                from the home three houses down

                yet I felt death by the handful
                emptying its load onto my lap
                skin absorbing the heavy loss
                it spilling from my chest, my
                eyes pouring pictures out, tacit words
                shooting, you were there:

in the op-shop hammock
hanging from the longest branch,
you near-winter rapt
lazing in the big sun
thin grey jumper, bottle of water
resting in the curve of your hip
the novel you had been talking about
sleeping on your full breast, and then
you were dead—the loss of your breath
felt in the stillness of the leaves.

                Death was not death that day
                even in autumn, when sunflowers
                refused to rise

but something like silence
and cloud-cover.

Sometimes I reach for your phantom body
as if I am trying not to fall.
I cannot breathe or speak
and this is what I want to say—

I might die, the heart ceding
to long stretches between go and go
the brain too tired to dictate to the heart
and no one, my love,
no one would hear my reaching.

Afterlife

-Ursula

Dear, dear winter,
who is to say heaven is not in the sea?
I walked, my feet wet in a maddening headwind,
there was a dog trying to round me up,
the seaweed piled in islands before me,
intermittent sprays of sun and the noise of the wind
and riotous waves, and the wet-suited kite surfer
splashing the sky. God knows to die means only
to move on with the invisible.[4] Imagine diving –
though stronger than diving—a perfect
acceptance of water, a perfect
forgiveness of earth's falling away.
Among fish, I could be eternal.

---

4   p 181

June 23rd

-Katherina

My face is longer than I remember /

                    maybe it's the mirror or the cut of my hair or the
                    clothes I've been wearing the past couple days

and then my eyes / my eyes
have faint bruises under
neath so they look longer too /

                        I see forty and seventy looking into a
                        mirror at fifty and seventy-two

I see lips full sans stretch so my chin
looks longer / my breasts are longer

            than they were last year / maybe I should try
            a new bra or maybe it's the clothes I've been
            wearing for days and days or maybe it's the
            mirror /

                    maybe the wine has gone to my head or
                    the tipping moon or the cut of my hair / but

the day is shorter than I remember.

'Soul cleaners'
xMel

Soya beaners
xD

'Sad ideas'
xM

Katherina
xD

So Caddy, I'm working on a poem for the next meeting and I feel like I should change it because of the rhythm but I'm having a moral issue with 'just add in a few stanzas' as Dolores said in our last meeting because it might take the blood and guts away from the poem. As a rule, editing seems to be a rejection of the moment and it's the moment in poetry that binds me to writing. Romantic, I know, but you said you edited the aeroplane poem at least ten times. Haven't you lost your core connection to it through the distancing and science? I'm pulling at my hair trying to grasp it all, also painting the study for the fourth time. As Lilith suggested, red.

Best, Katherina

Ciao Katherina. The house is so peaceful with Bruno asleep I can't bear to pick up the phone and speak, though that's how I'd love to dissect this with you. And besides, I'm actually editing now! Editing seems to get me closer to the core of my emotion, maybe the reliving of things, the re-evaluation from an imposed distance, letting it all flood back (like Dolores' vagina 😊 will we never stop talking about that poem?). Editing is my favourite part of writing, if only I could do it every day.

Happy painting,
Caddy

I Hope

-Caddy

...that you remember Johanna
and how you with your fingers so five-year-old deft
spent one sluggish day beading for her, glass orb
of sienna the showpiece on a pale child's neck.
Twice your pattern fell from the string
and there you were, hands and knees
crawling to corners, searching in cracks
until gathered, you restrung them with patience
such easy determination.

...that you realise the gentleness
of each flower you admired while alone in your head
thinking of her, and how just one stood perfect
as a beautiful accessory to Johanna's imperfect day.

...that you always dream about running the wrong way
through that blur of blue and yellow shirts
and sun-protective hats, those tiny obstacles
on your path to Johanna, the 3:05 *see ya*,
how you couldn't wait to see her again
as soon as you buckled in.

I hope that when you as a boy becoming a man
scared and free and open to life, fire fuelling hastiness
yet still that brooding, that seriousness
when you take a girl for that first time
in all her fragility, her quiet anxiety
that you remain as you were, thinking of her
thinking only of her.

Chilli-peppered

-Dolores

It's crazy how you love someone
more than chocolate in a golden wrapper,
smooth & hard, dissolving, deserving,
desiring of taste & suck
& then he discards you like that golden wrapper
after the chocolate's melted away
& every red car is his '86 Holden
passing you by along green green trees
& shopping trolleys abandoned,
naked without fruit or veg or dairy of any kind
& his favourite song is your favourite song
whenever it's on the radio even though you told him
a million times his taste in music was softer than shit
while yours nothing less than spicy sophistication
too hot to compare with defecation
& he would laugh his chuckled-laugh
your dreams still recreate & what's crazy
is that it's not security or company or cooking for two
or being late for whatever because you're in his arms...
& his eyes...& time has simply passed you by
along with your fear your innocence & clichéd phrases
that rode in that red car alongside organic feelings
of springtime every time he drove you
where he wanted to be, or his lips...or his love...
or his waiting for your homecoming
or how you fell asleep to his twitching toes, no!
It's crazy that everything you want back
is wrapped in a black, pubic mess so chocolate's
not what you want anymore because now your eyes
are stinging from sucking juice from a sliced chilli
& it's not even close to circumcised.

New Again

-Mel

New coins in my purse
new accent speaking the vowels of my name
new man, new bed, old panel van.

I'm trying hard to find something useful to say about your next Hyena's poem Mel but I can't find anything wrong with it, it's perfect in its Melish-way. Are we allowed to just say *yes yes yes* or do we have to be critical with all that we read? Can't a poem just *be*? Must it *be everything*?
Best to you, Katherina

Hahaha! That's nice of you say but I'm sure you can find SOMETHING wrong with it. I never know what to say at those meetings. Most of my comments on the printed out copies are nothing but ticks, double ticks and triple ticks. How about we start a trend of not caring.
x Mel

I don't care. Do you care?
Katherina

Don't care at all.
xMel

Dazzlers, I just had lunch with a friend who's going to live overseas for a year & wants to rent her cottage out as a holiday home in Burra. She's afraid no one will stay there & they'll be stretched for cash as the months drag on so I told her we'd rent it for a long weekend. That's it & now we do. Is five days with a houseful of women & wine & piles of poetry a long weekend? Say it's so. xD

Sounds like a fab idea and I want to make it happen, but I have to be careful with too many plans, still treading a bit of water with the health. My new theory is that it's the government making me sick, not these drastic barometric pressure changes. Can we make it during school break? Easier to get leave from work. / xLilith

I will move mountains to come, I will move mountains.
Katherina

I was JUST starting to feel like I needed a break from the sharehouse so it's perfect timing for me. Count me in whenever it is!
Cheers,
Mel

Hey everyone. After much poking and prodding 😊 Jean-Guy gave me the all clear for our weekend of poetry! I'll try to find a way to turn it into a long weekend but for now I'm tickled pink, or blue, or yellow with a plain old weekend. (Speaking of yellow, Mel, guess what I found in my car? Your yellow beanie!)
Bringing Bruno to Burra, of course,
Caddy

Dearest Cackle,
I'm sorry to be the wet tissue in the box but I won't be joining you. There's simply no way I can be away from Rupert overnight.
Ever yours, all of yours,
Ursula

Sorry about that, Ursula. I knew you'd have to say no and because of that it felt weird sending you the email without saying, 'Oh, Ursula, I know you won't be able to do this, sorry, but what about everyone else?' but then how weird would that have been if I did do that? Maybe I should've told you privately. We could've had this conversation first. I wish I knew what to say right now. I think I'm sticking my foot in it as I type. Tell me to shut up, would you?
xDolores

Dear Dolores,
By all means, don't upset yourself with this one. Sometimes I mind missing out on things, but this time I don't. Rupert and I go through waves of poignant love and stubborn frustration, and right now we are on a crest. Trust me when I tell you I am diving in fast and swimming in love before a storm comes in and drowns me.
x Ursula

Becoming Furry

-Ursula

At one-thirty in the morning I'm rustling awake,
        no surprise as you and I at five tonight
        fell exhausted together asleep.

We'd been fleshy in force;
so used to each other's scents and pores
it must've been last-ditch heat.

Flannel sheets don't suit our drive
so we lie in a soppy twin bed.

        (My back is wet against your chest.
        The moon is full against these walls.)

I twist and sigh, you squeeze me tight,
you sigh and writhe in return.
All the movement, the panting
the enormity of fucking, something old made new.

Now, as hair by hair we stick in sweat,
I want to fall back asleep to the barking dog
and dream we are wolves wet from a hunt,
worn from the zeal, asleep side by side for the sake
of survival, but know that it is something more.

Basket

-Lilith

You see my basket is full, though if I strain to lift it
by the two handles my lover once weaved into its base
my body might lose another piece of itself, so I'll sit
with its bounty instead. My body has proven that presence
is a sensual thing of tastes and swallows and valiant eruptions.
I have felt the audacity of splendour, its great seizures
of unattainability and I've housed it. Even during these last
precious months I have called my body a rose, something risen,
something blossomed, something witness to ocean and sky
and the touch of feather, so take heart, O take heart
that though I've filled my basket to the brim I am still filling it now,
recklessly warranting spillage for a perfect imperfect mess
and when it looks as though finally, yes, it might be enough
I'll keep going. Why would I ever want to stop?

Over It

-Mel

Look how you think
this is about you.

Watch how I walk
shoulders back.

Hi Lilith. I'm looking forward to your exhibition. Are you nervous? Gawd but I'm an insecure chook atm. I can't handle looking back at anything I've written and I've gained 5 kilos and become a blithering mess, so this email is coming from a bad place. Apologies in advance! I've been thinking about your critique and trying to work out how 'Over It' isn't specific enough when I claimed from the beginning I have a minimalist style, if saying I have a 'style' isn't a complete wank. The problem with the workshop is I feel everyone wants me to write a certain way, write longer poems, use metaphor, when I've never wanted to be a better poet and all I want to do is write. If I'm not writing for publication what good is editing? Isn't it enough that I use poetry to work heavy things out? I love the group but I don't have the same goals as any of you, I just like to write. And I think this has been bubbling away for the past couple of meetings, long-winded way to say sorry for my reaction at the Wheaty. Something burst and I couldn't stop it and I shouldn't've said you were bitter because I really didn't mean it AT ALL. I've no idea how I would handle living with MS or losing someone I love (or even being in love at all) and I think you're doing a top job teaching and writing and being the activist you are. You're so brave to risk those twitter rants on lack of representation in universities and then go to work AT A UNIVERSITY AS THE ONLY BROWN-SKINNED WOMAN IN YOUR DEPARTMENT! I could've used your example growing up, but I had other battles to fight. Anyway, you're fierce and I like that you always have something well thought out to say and your comments on my poems help more often than they hurt. I'm just taking everything personally these days. Winter's dragging on too long. Would you accept a cyber hug from me?
Cheers,
Mel

Mel / How I wish I could be more like you. I'll take your hug and throw in more and I will work to be extra sensitive to your needs. Look after yourself, yes? If you're having a difficult time, do call on me. I'm prone to cancelling last minute if we make a plan to meet out, but my door is always, always open. / xLilith

Broken Wings

-Dolores

I'm flying to my man at 2am
coz he knows how it is & always will be
he knows if it isn't him it's me
  all strung out & shining-like
  with booze breath oozing
  on his tongue touching mine
  flickering in our match stick light
  fluttering like some bruised angel
  yellow-skinned with hepatitis B.
I don't have to call, he hears my pain
howling like a siren down Hindley Street
& he's been my toilet bowl before
like he's been my rainbow early Christmas morning,
my lucky number winning on a big screen TV
like he's been my only friend
& in the end it's him holding my head
or me holding his cause that's just the way this love is
so I will fly with these broken wings
& I'll wrap myself in his ragged breast
coz our two halves make a shocking whole
& it's all I know
  all I know

Just a Passing Panic

-Dolores

I can't seem to find my soul!

Couldn't smell it in my sheets,
it wasn't in the toilet bowl,
looked for it in the city streets,
Damn my sneaky soul!

Dug in the desert & looked in a hole,
drank the bottle to the dregs,
it wasn't with my self-control
cause that ran down my legs.

Mmm. I taste it in your mouth.

Oh dear, a two-poem month for Dolores. It must be serious, but marriage? Surely you were kidding (she was kidding, right?). Do tread carefully with what you call 'love'. And Caddy, thank you for encouraging me to go to the No Wave reading. Wish you could have made it but I understand last minute things. Ursula, luckily, kept me company so I wasn't entirely lost. I most enjoyed knowing that when Jill Jones read, we were hearing fresh poems that no one else in the country even knew about. It does pay to live in Adelaide on occasion, doesn't it, cackle? / Lilith

Lilith, you're so anti-happiness when it comes to love which makes me love you more.
xxDolores

Not anti-happiness at all, Dolores, a façade, of course. To prove it I will tell you that I'm very much looking forward to our few days away in Burra. It will make me extremely *happy*, particularly if the rain lets up and the sun comes out. At the moment, however, day three of foul mood and counting. Getting an abstract ready for a conference in Budapest. Worried about it being accepted then having to deal with the long flight. How will my new old body cope? / Lilith

I'll join you in the foul mood Lilith but can no longer join any of you in Burra. Petrucio's forbidden me to go and I've long since forgotten how to challenge him. Can't seem to rise.
All the best, Katherina

I'm sorry to hear it,
Katherina. MEN MEN
MEN MEN MEN! I've
given up on them.
Celibacy has its
bonuses, like saving
so much money for
Uraguay! I haven't told
the others yet that I've
definitely decided to
go, in fact you're the
first person I've told
that it's official which
means I suppose it is.
Now wouldn't it be
excellent if you fucked
P off and came with
me?
xMel

Wouldn't that be
nice Mel though
a swimming
pool filled with
Sambuca would
be nice too
but I can't see
it happening.
Thank you
though. You'll be
sorely missed.
xKatherina

Hunger

-Katherina

The sun un-
fathomable, like

        flapjack syrup rays   butter sizzle
        beaded skin

Why say it is the moon?
        (lune   luna   *tic*)

It is lunch:
I love you, you say
        I do   say the sun is the moon

           say I am you   marmalade / mama laid

moon cheese   soup tease   slap me.

What You Had

-Mel

You had bottles of Meerlust
Scarlatti sonatas and Lord Byron;

I wore black, reflecting my heart
      which you did not have.

Now I know we've talked about other people joining us before but I just met the coolest woman who some of you know. She's very clever. Anyway, we got to talking and I told her about our group and she asked if she could join. It's Autumn Laing.
x Mel

Hi everyone. I feel it's safe for me to say that you all have become precious to me as individuals but even more so as an entity, as a cackle, as a group of women I've come to need and love.
I can't imagine anyone coming into our group and trying to fit in. It seems we've already been through the hiccoughs of dating and now it's as if we're living together, and so swiftly, too! We know who buys the Swiss cheese and who steals the mint slices, and we know who leaves the empty toilet rolls on the floor next to the toilet, who swears when the relatives come over and who has to be asked twice for the rent money. We know who does and doesn't do the dishes after a dinner party (thank you Dolores and thank you Lilith for all of your effort in Burra 😊) and we accept it all because it's true love.
If August joined, if anyone joined, it would be difficult accepting she might leave the door open when she shits. (Sorry but you know I have a baby so there is always the possibility of poop in my metaphors.)
No, no, shaking my head no,
Caddy

Dear us / Enjoying a bout of good health so I'm taking full advantage, even rode my bike to the shops to pick up veggies, and lucky it's a flat ride because it's a mad spring wind indeed. My bicycle and I soldier on. Sorry, Mel, but I've no interest in adding to our group for the same reasons as Caddy. I know Autumn Laing fairly well, she used to go those Lee Marvin readings back when dinosaurs roamed, and I really don't think it would work. / xLilith

Yeah & no one's mentioned we told Daisy Buchanan she couldn't join—we can't say no to one person & yes to another.
xxD

Tell Autumn we're sorry Mel, and Ursula, I've made a beef and spinach stew to give Rupert strength but that's only a disguise, it's really to give you strength. Don't tell him though.
Best wishes to all of you, Katherina (who is smoking again.)

Dear Katherina,
That's so thoughtful of you. Bring it around any time. I'll have tea set up in the garden, and if I still haven't had a decent night's sleep, I might steal a cigarette off you.
Yours lovingly,
Ursula

Slow Crab

-Ursula

You said you wanted a love like sleep

       but remember the commotion
       the lake was sunk to quarter size
       it had horrible raw banks of clay
       that smelled of raw rottenish water.[5]

       You kissed me as they pulled the bodies out
       dripping and stinking of their endless tragedy
       her hands gripping his throat.

Why should love be like sleep?[6]

---

5   p 178
6   p 174

Dearest Hyenas,

I sent this month's poem to my sister in Tokyo who said our poetry group sounded beautiful and I told her it was impossible for me to ever explain just how truly beautiful it is. She told me she was hoping I'd given up the footnotes by now and was disappointed with 'Slow Crab', said she wished I could separate myself from the text, that perhaps I feel defined by my 'character'. She argued my complexity and said she worried about my self-worth. I told her Rupert is sick *for fucksake* and it is not Lawrence I am living for but Rupert, Rupert, only myself and Rupert. I watch him get paler and thinner and weaker and sadder every single day and yes, sometimes there is sun, intermittently, and when there is we are both sated in warmth, but it takes energy to be happy on the days we struggle together and so I must look to other sources. I look to you. As always, she apologised; she is my sister and arguments occur as frequently as the tide comes in. As a way to make amends she wrote a poem about the same night and used footnotes. I think it's marvellous and I asked her if I could show it to you.

Yours faithfully,

Ursula

Love and Death

-Gudrun

So unreasonable, their drowning
      her hands tight around his throat, the night seemed large and vacuous[7],
      there was confusion, howling, reflecting lights disorienting boundaries
      of water and stars. I told myself they couldn't be dead, too extravagant
      and sensational[8] and you were gilled as far as I could tell spending
      minutes underwater—it was then I knew I loved you, saying *there's*
      room under that water there for thousands[9] as if heaven were not at all in
      the sky but below the surface of what we know
                              floating and tethered to the drowned.

---

7   p 168
8   p 168
9   p 172

Dearest Gudrun,

But your poem is no less 'you' than any of your others. Can't you see that you're still there only so is Lawrence? I think you make a valid point and we could certainly have a good go at it next time we see one another, but I will tell you then as I tell you now that I believe history is one truth you cannot escape, and if there is no truth in poetry, where does that leave us? Reap your history and sow the poem, Prune. At any rate, the women loved it, and your comments created quite a buzz so it's unanimous: when you are next in Adelaide you must come to an RWH meeting. What a wonderful cackle of hyenas we are, like family, and it's precisely because you are my true family that I am going to have the last word in telling you that I do not believe I am limiting myself; I am not a closed book. Your sister forever and ever,

Ursula

Bianca

-Katherina

Where lies home
      here   (and husband alone)
      there   (and sister secrets
          pouring through the corridor
              fingers fitting like hair clasps)

My husband lies, says he's   home
      I'm drunk on wine   *(no, I'm fine)*
      and hum so deep, my throat it moans
      (and sister roams, garden pond
       fingers fit
      like hair clasps).

Hey, Katherina. I promise you I cried when I read your poem. I can see how much you miss your sister. I have such strong memories of my brother Benjy and I miss him every day. With his disability it seemed no one in our family had the patience for him, but I loved him and I cared for him. Do you think memory would exist without childhood? And our concept of home too, doesn't home need childhood? And can poetry exist without memory and therefore home and therefore childhood? I've been getting a collection of poems together for the Adelaide Festival / Wakefield Press award for unpublished manuscripts and editing all the poems I've written since we moved here, and even though they're about my here and now, there's memory everywhere! Water, forests, landmarks I've claimed as my own, people I've loved, the path I took to school and the scent of the foliage. I've had so many 'homes' in my adult life that I think I need to be rooted again (in the American sense I mean, actually going through a sexual slump right now but that's a whole other story). Is Adelaide a place I can set down roots? Sometimes I dream of Mississippi and my return. I'd take Jean-Guy and the boys and make it our home and it'd feel pure. My daughter is there. I would hold her and tell her I'm sorry a million times and never let go. Then my older brother would kill me. This is not an exaggeration.
Wishing I could hug you right now,
Caddy

I can't get into 'home' right now. I'm tender from some difficult days and terrible nights. Literally. Tender. Petrucio's enjoying the current global swing towards normalised racism and we argue all the time. He is an arse. And men will always kill women. Is winter almost over? xKatherina

Cherished friend, it's mid-October. We're well into spring, which is a good thing if we're to believe that spring brings hope. Let's hope for strength and love and that Petrucio comes to his senses, or maybe catches a bug that makes him sleep all day long. You don't sound good. Are you safe? I say if you can't be safe in your own home, darlin, it isn't a home worth having. YOU MUST KEEP YOURSELF SAFE. Please let me know if there's anything you need, anything at all.
xxCaddy

Mississippi

-Caddy

You offer me crab apples, lightning bugs, a red pick-up with a confederate flag
passing black men walking for miles, the gentle roll of the flat road
leading to some other county. I wrap the warmth of my body
around your great rivers, my hips and elbows curving with each bend.
I let clear water from creeks splash my skin, hold white pebbles
in my hand then pack them away for a time like now.

I smell you, Mississippi, petals of honeysuckle wet like my own,
your name a soft stammer on my tongue, like a lover's.
I romanticise you as wild and random; native honeybees
flirt in the juices of a full-bosomed magnolia tree
where in its branches the trill of a mockingbird, and over there
the sound of someone's pleasure at three in the afternoon.

Sassparilla, Chickasaw, loblolly pine, dead skunk.

I can hear your guitar and your fiddle, your children and your unborn babies
the old stories—of mammies, of the fields, of dead brothers.

What is Left

-Lilith

Last night it rained, the grass reclaiming the yard
with pompous green overspill while leaves lay patches
of yellow blankets and die. There is toast, coffee, a tragedy:
The Taming of the Shrew, somehow tagged a comedy.

You held the book for months in your hands, Shakespeare's sonnets
perched on your lips that moved quick and small, the fragile skin
of a newfound love blustering in a newer wind.

The morning after the stone-faced scowl of the Berlin Wall
was smashed to pieces the dust settled on our new world.
Everyone celebrated, tongues devouring tongues in a fetish of youth
and democracy on any street, in any café, and you were reading
this red book, you dog-eared these thin pages, and I can feel your fingerprints.

Other days it is the taste of tarragon, the green knit scarf
we used to share, mindlessly walking to the passenger side of our car.

Grim Reapers
xD

'Ballerinas'
xMel

Been thinking of you today, Lil, wondering if it's better that death comes quickly so you don't have to go through the mourning while the person you love is still alive. Like when Eve had cancer, didn't you miss her while she was still alive? Seems a shitty thing to have to deal with. Today's my mom's birthday—she would've been 50. Same age as you. I kinda want to be 50 now so I can feel like an adult but I'm too afraid of getting old. I can't help wondering what my mom would've been like if she'd lived. I wonder what she would've made of me. Nobody knows this & don't go telling it but I pray pretty much every night. I don't believe in God, just pray. I started doing it the year she died. I know it's not for everyone & I don't want to come off as some missionary-type but I've been thinking about you & how hard things have been for you so I've decided to pray for you too. I know how you feel about religion but this is beyond that if you know what I mean. You can tell me to stop if you want. xDolores

Ah, Dolores, a sad day for you today. I send you warmth and deep reflection. Thank you for your thoughts and prayers. I'm settling into this new life of mine, alone and ill, and I'm finding once there is acceptance, life isn't so bad. By all means, keep praying for me. Perhaps that's what's been working. / xLilith

I feel a little uncomfortable about Lilith's last
poem bringing up Katherina's story and you, my
friend, are the EXACT person I need to talk to
about this. What did you think of her whipping
out *Taming of the Shrew* like that?
Cheers,
Mel

Dear Mel,
To be honest, I wondered when
we'd start using each other's stories
to make better sense of our own.
I believe our lives are enmeshed
now, and this goes beyond poetry.
When you are happy, Mel, I am
happy, and when you are sad I'm
sad for you; you affect me. If our
pasts affect us today then your past
and Caddy's past and Katherina's
past affects me, too. We are such
a conglomerate of the women
who came before us, and the more
we know about one another the
more that truth becomes evident
to me. We need to keep examining
ourselves through the stories we
tell and the stories other women
tell, and I know my thinking might
not be so popular with those
outside of literature, but within the
fold, don't we hope, most of all, to
speak to one another?
Yours in honesty and love,
Ursula

But it's Shakespeare's story, not Katherina's!
(Yours in mild indignation and love,)
xMel

> Mel, I disagree: it *is* her story, and
> yet her story still goes on without
> Master Shakespeare. Now it's
> playing a role in Lilith's poem.
> Intertextuality for all.
> xxUrsula

I see your point but I'm not convinced.

> Write a poem with Dolores in it, just
> for fun. See if it shapes your story.
> Yours in the perfect sun,
> Ursula

Woe is me everyone. I tried to have a productive day
to take my mind off less pleasant thoughts—a dead
mother causes lifelong grief & it would've been her
50th birthday today—but I threw it all in & took my
daughter to a cemetery, any cemetery & we placed
flowers on some woman's grave. When I came home
I thought I'd be productive again & write about what
we did but it's not working. Now I've had a few wines
& a cone & I'm looking over old poems, letting my buzz
do its thing & here I am attaching one to you Hyenas. I
wrote it years ago when Bea's dad left us & every time
I come back to it I sort of love it but hate it more. It's
not an RWH poem—just want your first impressions if
any of you are in the mood. Really I need to hear from
you before I go to bed so write back & tell me you've
no time for non-Hyena poems or whatever, just write
back. (Mel, you'll see a tiny homage to you right near
the end.) xDolores

Seasonal

-Dolores

You weren't the first snowflake or the last
& I was no fresh stalk of grass, but still I was bladed
as if I was born with a need to defend myself
& point my tongue, shine my sword, kill you while you slept.

When we collided, I fell into the stinging wetness
of your snowy self, froze when you swaddled my skin.
I gave in. You multiplied, made it your duty to protect
by smothering my covering of a green-growth life-force
that wanted to be left alone. I began to wane.

Then one day it was only you, piles of you for miles of you
& you so grand I couldn't see anything left of what was me.
& that was how it happened. When the sun came out
you cried. You felt its presence compacting
so you began insisting I soak you up completely.
You wanted to drown me, so afraid you would die
but I refused to cough up water. I never even gurgled.

That was when I became seasonal, realised I needed change
to make things grow, realised one day I might forget snow,
might discover the sky, fly over mountains, find a new land,
new man, new panel van, winter at the beach.

Lament

-Mel

your voice washing over my skin
dirty with possibilities
>adrenaline
>and disgust

>there were raindrops in my hair;
>it seemed an endless month of rain
>and you –

Lately

-Ursula

The seagulls separate sea and sand
through touch and taste and instinct,
how I separate the boundaries of you.

Lately when I want you
it could be from across the outdoor table,
iron lattice indentations and toast crumbs on skin,
scent of sliced oranges, pear tree parrots gibbering away,
  the inexplicable squint of your eyes
   as if everything is a wonder
    and a nuisance.

It could be in the chair,
the square where the afternoon sun shines in,
a green and pink knitted rug on your wasted legs,
a fallen book of Ezra Pound
  or when you ask for help to rise from the toilet,
  when you whimper in the shadowless night.

Lately I want you
in your greatest trepidation,
in your still and brooding acquiescence,
vulnerable as a baby just coming into the world,[10]
helpless as a man
   leaving in lovely silence.

---

10 p 174

Hola Dolores. I can't tell you how much fun we had with you and Bea. What a protector she is, holding onto Bruno's hand as he toddled along the trail, yelling to Max to come back, he was too far ahead. She's clearly grown up with love. I was thinking we should do it again, get out in the shimmering eucalypt where our own yapping balances the magpie's warble. That walk made me realise I'm ready to get back into shape, lose a little baby weight. I've decided I'm going to spend the summer exploring the green nooks and crannies of Adelaide, and wasn't Anstey Hill just a perfect way to start! What do you think? Should we do it again?
Calves still aching,
Caddy

Just told Bea the plan. Should've seen her smile. I'm thinking before Christmas & this time bring dogs. xxD

Oh, I just wrote a dog poem today, thought I'd send it to the Hyneas! ☺ xxCaddy

Thank you Lilith for that stack of old Islands and Southerlys. Fiona Wright must've been on a roll, she's everywhere in them and good on her. I've spent a lot of time asking myself 'what can poetry do?' because it's the meetings and the discussions and the emails we send and the friendship that's mattered most to me this year but today I had an aha birthday moment so I spent this 42nd celebration reading through the journals with a bottle of Cab Sav from the Coonawarra (2009 was a very bad year) and I've decided to start sending off my poems because hey, what if it worked? The courage it takes is frightening and invigorating so now that I've thought of it I've got to do it but what do I say in the bio they ask for when I haven't any publications? Another thing is I want to join you at the Black Lives Matter rally. I one hundred percent believe in the movement but I've also got a lot to shout about and crammed into a mob of angry people fighting for justice seems as good a time as any. And another thing is I've been thinking that if I could linger on a single letter long enough to communicate how I feel right now it would be a P. I'm trying to work out what that means.
xKatherina

But darling, you are a member of Rhymes with Hyenas, surely that is enough? In all seriousness, why don't you draw on your style or talk about what motivates your structure or who your influences are? Be uniquely Katherina.
And you know forty-two is a special age, yes? Perhaps P is for Paramount or Powerful. Why don't you meet Mel and me at the train station on Saturday at 10:30 where the benches are. I'll have a large sign we can lift together. / xxLilith

How is this for paramount: I've decided to leave Petrucio. Is your offer to stay in the spare room still available? I need something bigger than a large sign to grab hold of while I'm feeling P-for-powerful, let me hold onto a yes. Yes?
xKatherina

Gardening

-Katherina

Call a thing by its name:
  dripping tap and
  rusted chair,
  sunflower seedling
  vegetable patch
  decapitated statue of naked man

     Katherina   Katherina

      in black gumboots and summer dress
      stinging nettle erupting from suburban soil

     Adelaide   Adelaide

      and last week's heatwave
      decapitated statue of naked man

Decapitated statue of naked man
  watering can by
  rainwater tank
  peeling paint
  old fence
  tomato trellis, trawler

     Katherina   Katherina

      in gardening gloves
      decapitated statue of naked man.

Eve's Earthly Sin

-Lilith

1. *Freedom*

Eve stole an apple from the fresh fruit market
just slipped it inside her black shoulder bag.
Freedom was the word she sought
because I can she said.
And passing through the park she passed
many times a week
this day she stopped and sat in sun
on green under blue by a tree.
It was there she tanned her nipples brown
it was there she ate the apple red
so red the blood and tongue the lips
how red her eyes when closed
and as a cloud devoured the sun
Eve felt cold, and bare.

2. *Disgrace*

With apple skin caught between her teeth
Eve went to the Salvation Army.
Salvation caught her searing eyes
disgrace caught in her throat.
A four-dollar dress covered her arms
and covered her legs and covered
her chest and rose to her neck
sheltering the mole that pulsed
with the heat of her blood. Her black
dress fell to her ankles, covering her fish tattoo.
The sheer scarf matched the dress:
black just goes with black.
Eve tied a scarf around her head.
Eve hung her head in shame.

3. Yummm

With apple core rotting in kitchen bin
Eve went to the Central Markets—
only Babylon could be so loud,
a butcher's mother beam so proud.
Colours and scents signalled a gossip Eve's nose
and eyes understood, and her heart fell praying
on the floor for what clearly was fertility.
O antipasto! O stinking fish!
You shape of zucchini and flashes
of orange! Flowering artichoke
and sister half-fig! Eve's volta
flipped, did a serendipitous jig.
Yummm echoed in her head;
grumble rolled in her stomach.

4. Grow

With apple seeds in her cast-off scarf
Eve planted a garden,
such a small square
such deep earth, big enough
to cake the cracks of her fingerprints
and contemplate a rainwater tank,
to hoist her skirt up over her thighs
and roll up those sleeves, unbutton that top
to run the scarf between her breasts
catching the sweat, then on her brow and below
the backs of her dripping knees
where Eve celebrated dirt and bees.
Guilt is a useless word she thought
grow is what she said.

Trees (Burra)

-Caddy

Inland, and hours removed from the sea, a white tree
bathes in day, stores saliva and grows from a hardened floor.

We follow it through the morning's glare on the glass window
until it passes, the radio tied to the city's wires linking music to sky

long since crackled and given up. We drive on to the hidden creek
rest under a hundred-year-old gumtree I believe still believes.

Proud earth laps at my shoe so that later, at the antique shop
where I find an enormous teal pot, I leave a mud print on the rug.

Then, evening, city-bound and radio back, the DJ's playing Gurrumul.
I don't know Yolngu but I think the song's about sunset through the branches.

Hello lovely hyenas! I had a HUGE cry after my farewell party last night. You are the most encouraging and thoughtful friends I've ever had the pleasure of loving. As Caddy suggested a million years ago, next meeting at my place, in Uruguay, baby!
xxMel

The Street between Two Streets

-Mel

It was leaving the pub
and one of us singing;
how the rest of us joined in.

It was the moon,
the moon and a gumtree.

Acknowledgements

This manuscript has a long lifespan, begun almost two decades ago and resuscitated every few years. Many of its poems were published in journals that no longer exist and I thank those literary journals—I thank all literary journals—for insisting on publishing poetry in an unforgiving market. Thanks especially to the editors of these: *Cordite, DB, Famous Reporter, Griffith Review, Literary Mama, Parenting Express, Poetrix, Polestar, Small Packages, Strange4, TEXT, Westerly.* Also thanks to the editors of these anthologies: *Fingers and Tongues* (Paroxysm Press), *Forked Tongues* (Wakefield Press), *Poetry d'Amour 2013: Love Poems for Valentine's Day* (WA Poets), *Ten Years of Things that Didn't Kill Us* (Paroxysm Press). Thinking this book would never be published, part of 'Sea Dragons' was used for another poem which was published in 2017's Newcastle Poetry Prize Anthology, *The Crows in Town* and will be reprinted in my next poetry book, *Alternative Hollywood Ending* (Wakefield Press). I'm so grateful to Shane Strange at Recent Work Press for taking a risk on this book, for seeing the vision had worth when the writing hadn't yet gotten there, and to Penelope Layland for her efforts to get the writing 'there'. What an impressive editor—I'm here to sing your praises. Thanks to Mike Ladd and Cathy Brooks for including 'The Street between Two Streets' in their visual art project and subsequent small publication *Signs of Life in Bowen Street.* The first draft of this book was written with help from the Richard Llewellyn Deaf and Disability Arts fund, and I'm incredibly grateful for it and for all of the art they fund. Likewise I want to thank Red Room Poetry for gifting me Writer in Residence at the Tin Cat Café as part of the Café Poets program during that first draft—love your work then and still love it today. And thank you, Claire Graham, for supporting my time there, as well. I miss the Tin Cat. Lots of us do. Thank you to 12th International DH Lawrence Conference and Flinders University's Shadow of the Precursor conference, where I presented papers on this project and was granted the opportunity to read some of the poems to my peers. Thanks to the JM Coetzee Centre for Creative Practice at the University of Adelaide, where academics continually inspire me. Thank you to all the poets and writers who helped along the way: The KPT's Lucy Alexandre, Kimberly Mann, Shen, Bel Shenk and Tim Sinclair; my Siswas Cassy Flanagan Willanski, Cathoel Jorss and Kerryn Tredrea; Edit When Sober's Alison Flett and Rachael Mead; Susan Hawthorne and other perceptive friends Gay Lynch, Anna Solding and Julia Winefield. Enormous love and thanks to Dash for inspiring the love poems and my kids for allowing me to fully inhabit Caddy's domesticity: motherhood rocks with you three in tow. Respect and gratitude to JM Coetzee, William Faulkner, DH Lawrence, Vladimir Nabokov, William Shakespeare and whichever man it was in the Jewish community, over a thousand years ago, who first began telling stories about Lilith. The women created by these men have touched me deeply, each at different times in my life. Respect and gratitude to *all women* in literature who've touched me, to *all women* who've touched me, to *all women*.

This book was written on the unceded lands of the Kaurna people in Tarntanya Adelaide. I thank the custodians for their care of the land and the elders for the stories they keep alive.

Printed in Australia
AUHW020905200921
352373AU00002B/2

9 780645 008982